Your Body and
Your Health

Schofield & Sims Limited Huddersfield.

The Body is a Wonderful Machine

Published in the UK in 1994 by
Schofield & Sims Limited, Huddersfield, England.

0 7217 5005 2

Birth

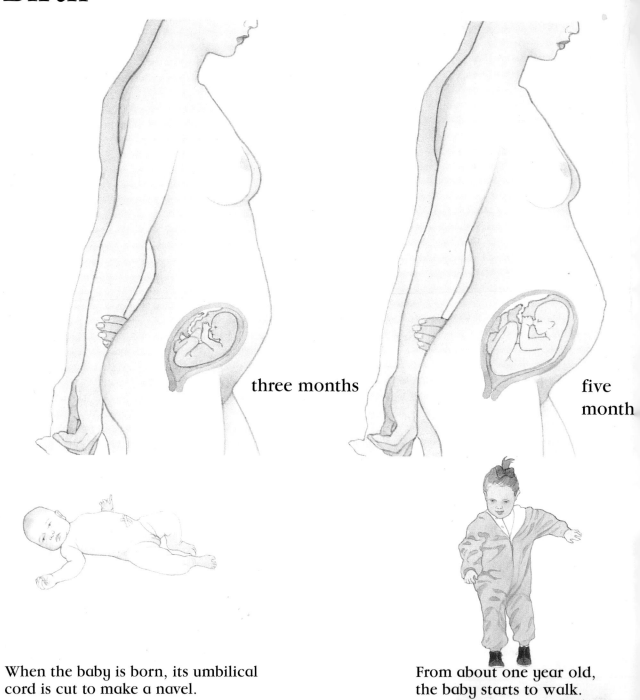

three months

five month

When the baby is born, its umbilical cord is cut to make a navel.

From about one year old, the baby starts to walk.

4

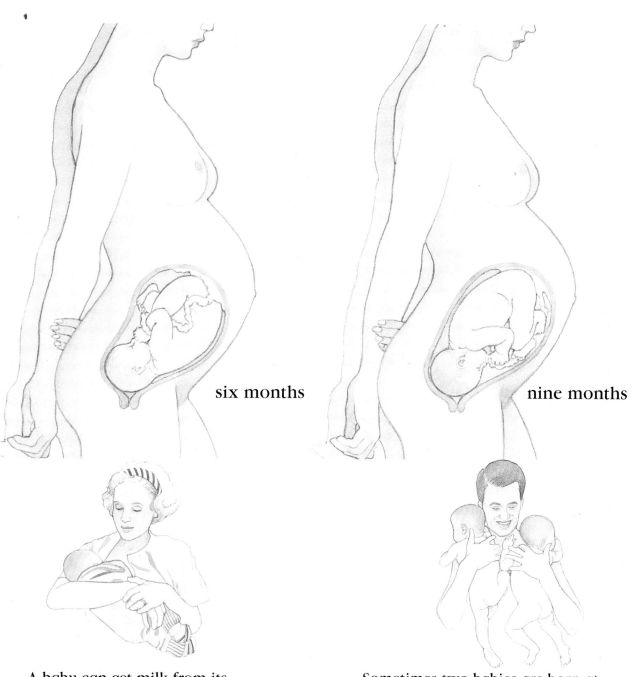

six months

nine months

A baby can get milk from its mother to help it grow.

Sometimes two babies are born at the same time. They are called twins.

5

Skin

Skin covers our bodies. It is smooth, flexible and *waterproof*. It protects us from the sun, dirt and *germs*.

The skin's colour depends partly on the climate. Where there is more sunshine, skin is usually darker.

Animals have a skin, too. A rhinoceros's skin is much thicker than ours and a snake's skin is made of scales.

Hair has its roots embedded in the *scalp*. When your hair falls out, new hair grows to replace it.

Nails protect our fingers and toes. Our nails are not as well developed as those of some animals because we do not use our nails as much.

Muscles and Bones

Under our skin we have muscles that enable us to walk, run and jump. Muscles move the bones in our skeleton. Our bones grow bigger and heavier as we get older.

When we contract our muscles, we can feel them under our skin. They become shorter, bigger and harder. Then we can make them relax.

There are more than 30 muscles in the face. They open and close our eyes, move our jaws, and let us pull faces.

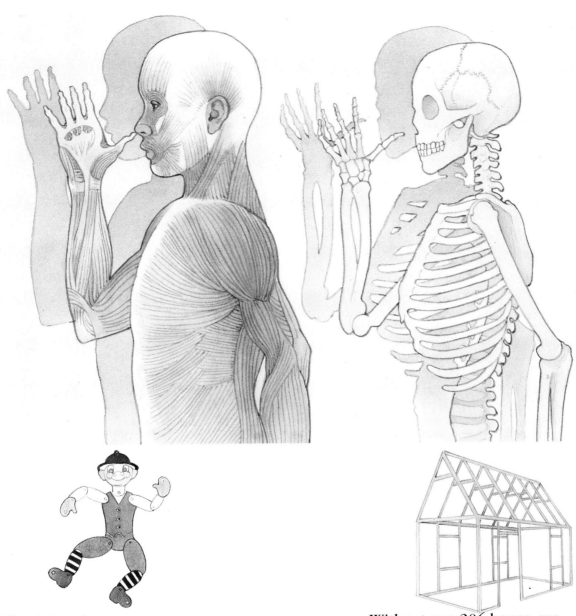

The *joints* that connect our bones to each other allow us to bend our fingers, arms and legs and to turn our heads.

Without our 206 bones, we would not be able to walk upright. The skeleton is the *framework* of the body.

9

The Brain

Like a computer, the brain controls our bodies, our movements and our thoughts. It also makes sure that all our organs, such as the heart, are working properly.

It is our brain that lets us remember the things we have learnt.

The brain controls our emotions, our laughter and our tears.

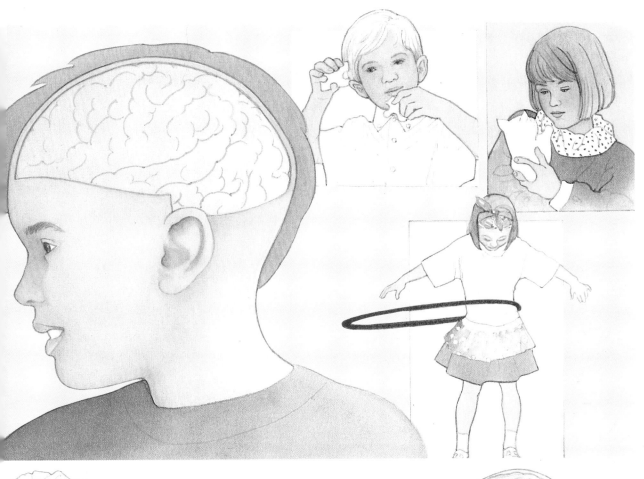

Even when we are asleep, the brain continues working. It makes sure the heart is beating, that we are breathing properly and that our digestive system is working.

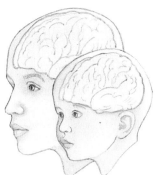

An adult's brain weighs about 1.4 kilograms which is four times as heavy as a baby's brain.

The Five Senses

The eyes, the ears, the tongue, the nose and the skin are the organs of the five senses: sight (with the eyes), hearing (with the ears), taste (with the tongue), smell (with the nose) and touch (with the skin). All these senses help us to experience the world outside.

Our eyes are protected by eyelids, eyelashes and eyebrows.

The eardrum inside an ear acts like the skin of a drum. Sounds make the eardrum *vibrate*.

Parts of our tongue, called taste
buds, enable us to recognise four
tastes – sweet, salty, bitter and sour.

Thanks to our skin, we know the
difference between cold and heat,
and between dryness and dampness.

The Lungs

We need to breathe to live. Air goes in through the nose or mouth, and travels down the throat until it gets to the lungs, which are well protected by the ribs.

When we breathe in, our lungs inflate like a balloon. They deflate when we breathe out.

Divers carry cylinders of oxygen to breathe under water.

The Heart

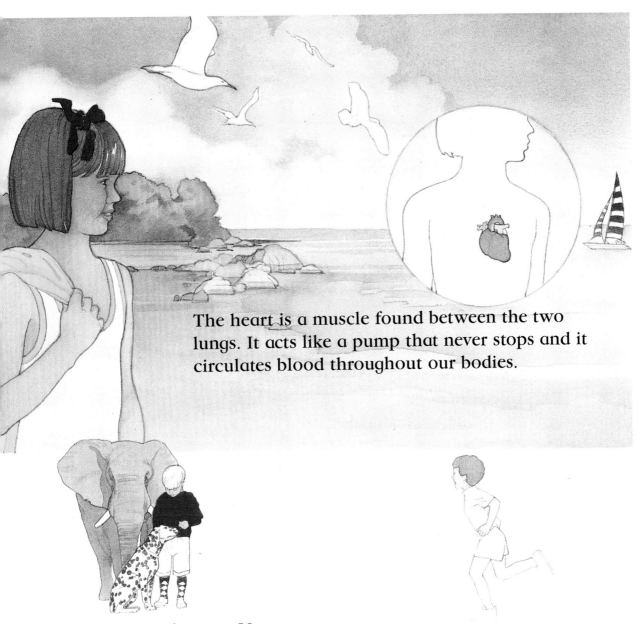

The heart is a muscle found between the two lungs. It acts like a pump that never stops and it circulates blood throughout our bodies.

A child's heart beats between 80 and 100 times per minute, as does a dog's heart. An elephant's heart beats only 20 times a minute.

When we run, we breathe heavily and our hearts beat quicker and more strongly.

Healthy Eating

To grow and be in good health,
we need to eat and drink several times a day.
A healthy, varied diet gives
our bodies everything
they need to
function normally.

Meat, fish and eggs are good for strong bodies and muscles.

Dairy products, such as milk, yoghurt and cheese, make teeth and bones stronger.

Bread, cereals and potatoes give us energy.

Fruit and vegetables contain vitamins that protect us against *germs*.

Good Digestion

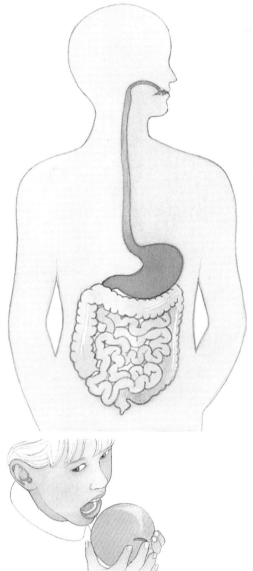

We need to eat to live but, in order for food to be used by our bodies, it has to be changed by some of our organs – our digestive system.

The digestive system begins in the mouth. Our teeth cut and mash food into pieces which are small enough to be swallowed.

The stomach is a sort of big pouch where solid food is made into a liquid.

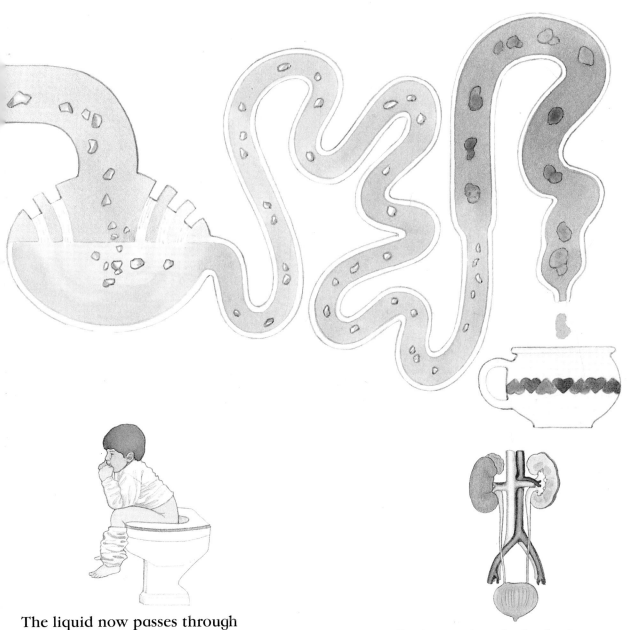

The liquid now passes through the intestines, which keep only what is useful for the body. The remainder is *excreted*.

The water that the body does not need is turned into urine by the kidneys, then *excreted*.

Dangers

While you are growing up, you have to learn to protect yourself from danger on the road, in the garden or around the house.

Do not drink any liquid unless you know it is safe. Some liquids can poison you.

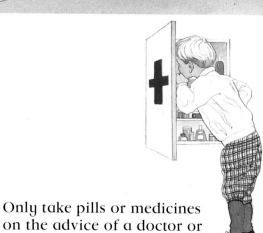

Only take pills or medicines on the advice of a doctor or parent.

Do not touch electrical plugs or *appliances*. They can be very dangerous.

Animals are not toys. Even when they seem very gentle, do not tease them.

Healthy Life

To live a healthy and happy life, we need games and exercise. We also need to have good friends, to read books and to listen to music, so that we can learn about and understand the world we live in.

It is important to keep our bodies and hair clean. We also need to brush our teeth to avoid *tooth decay*.

Sleep allows our bodies to rest, grow and stay healthy. That is why we often sleep a lot when we are ill.

Germs sometimes attack us and cause colds, flu, tonsillitis and other illnesses.

To protect us against such illnesses as measles, whooping cough or mumps, we need to have *vaccinations*.

Did You Know?

We start to lose our 20 milk teeth at about the age of 6. Then we grow 28 teeth that are bigger and stronger so that we can chew food better.

When we are cold, we get goose-pimples and our hair stands on end.

More than half of our body is made up of water.

Some people cannot tell the difference between red and green. We say that they are 'colour blind'.

Twin brothers or twin sisters grow together in their mother's womb. They often look very much alike.

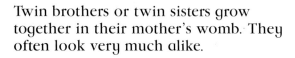

Our bones are strong, but they can be broken. If we break a bone we may have to wear a plaster cast while the broken bone joins up again.

The voice can be so high-pitched that the sound can break a glass.

When we sneeze, air comes out of our noses at 160 kilometres an hour!

Our bodies convey our feelings and emotions, even if we do not realise it.

We dream every night and sometimes have nightmares, even if we do not remember the next day.

Glossary

Appliance
A piece of equipment, such as a kettle, which is used for a particular task.

Excrete
To force out.

Framework
Building blocks, e.g. in a house the framework holds up the roof.

Germ
A tiny organism, invisible to the eye, that causes illness. Bacteria are germs. A virus is a germ.

Joint
Where two or more bones join together to make a strong hinge, e.g. knee or elbow.

Scalp
Skin on the head that contains hair.

Tooth decay
The crumbling of a tooth often started by food lodged in a break in the protective enamel.

Vaccination
A kind of medicine that protects the body from certain illnesses. Some vaccinations are given as injections. Others can be swallowed.

Vibrate
To move backwards and forwards very rapidly.

Waterproof
Anything that keeps out water.